Contents

Welcome to Rigby Navigator

Giving you the Right Tools for the Job

Rigby Navigator is specially designed to help you unlock the potential of guided reading. It makes guided reading easy to manage and enjoyable for both teachers and children. The programme provides books for fiction, non-fiction, poetry and plays for 7–11 year olds. *Navigator* also has the flexibility to be used alongside your existing guided reading resources.

Navigator Fiction

Rigby Navigator Fiction has been written to help you deliver creative and effective guided reading sessions for all your pupils. Each book contains three short stories, tailor-made for guided reading sessions, so they are the right length and at the right interest level.

Each book is supported by its own Teaching Guide. The clear teaching focus for each session will save you valuable preparation time.

Developing Comprehension Skills

Guided reading is an important part of children's literacy experience. It is an opportunity for them to engage with the reading process and to discuss their thoughts with the teacher and with other children. It helps ensure that they experience a broad variety of texts, genres and vocabulary. Guided reading in KS2 helps children to build on their literal comprehension and factual recall skills. In addition, it supports the development of the higher level skills of inference, deduction, justification and evaluation. Throughout the *Rigby Navigator* sessions you will find questions, tailored to each book, to help children acquire and develop these skills.

Implementing Guided Reading

All schools have different timetables and priorities, and guided reading should be considered as part of a whole literacy programme. Many schools find it most effective to include some guided reading time in the main literacy session, with extra daily guided reading sessions. *Rigby Navigator* provides plenty of materials for groups to work on while the teacher works with a particular set of children.

You can choose your own route through the material, so that you can personalise your sessions to meet particular groups' needs.

Making the most of Guided Reading

Each session in *Rigby Navigator* details the renewed Framework objectives, as well as success criteria. These can be shared with the children at the start of each session, to make sure that they know what the session will cover. Recapping the success criteria at the end of the session will encourage children to evaluate their own performance.

Valuable information can be accrued during guided reading about children's application of essential reading skills and strategies. Each session contains one or more QCA Assessment Focuses for Reading, to help ensure that you have a clear picture of each child's progress.

Support for Planning

Each session in *Rigby Navigator* lists the renewed Framework objectives covered in that session; and these are summarised in the table opposite. Charts showing which of the renewed Framework objectives are and are not covered for a given year are available in the *Rigby Navigator* Programme Handbooks.

Differentiation

The wide range of ability levels in the classroom adds to the time needed to prepare for effective guided reading. *Navigator* Teaching Guides offer teachers flexible routes through each story, so that each guided reading session can be differentiated, allowing you to meet every group's needs.

Models for Writing

The short stories also serve as perfect exemplar texts for children's own writing. The Guides have a strong focus on writing, drawing on the essential link between reading and writing.

Primary Framework Teaching Objectives

This table shows the objectives, taken from the renewed Framework for literacy, covered by the guided reading sessions in this book. You will find abbreviated versions of these objectives on the Teaching Guide pages, and a chart showing the coverage of these objectives for all books in this level in the Programme Handbook.

Spooky or What? – Mystery stories

		Session 1 / 2	Session 3 / 4
Time and Tide by Paul Stewart	Renewed Framework objectives	**Focus on 3rd Person Accounts** **Y3 Strand 7: 2** Infer characters' feelings in fiction and consequences in logical explanations **Y3 Strand 8: 3** Identify features that writers use to provoke readers' reactions	**Focus on Plot** **Y3 Strand 1: 3** Sustain conversation, explain or give reasons for their views or choices **Y3 Strand 7: 1** Identify and make notes of the main points of section(s) of text **Writing** **Y3 Strand 10: 1** Signal sequence, place and time to give coherence
The Girl in the Red Coat by Sean Taylor	Renewed Framework objectives	**Focus on Significant Aspects of the Story** **Y3 Strand 3: 2** Actively include and respond to all members of the group **Y3 Strand 8: 3** Identify features that writers use to provoke readers' reactions	**Focus on 1st Person Accounts** **Y3 Strand 7: 1** Identify and make notes of the main points of section(s) of text **Y3 Strand 7: 2** Infer characters' feelings in fiction and consequences in logical explanations **Writing** **Y3 Strand 9: 1** Make decisions about form and purpose, identify success criteria and use them to evaluate their writing
Horses of the Winter Night by David Clayton	Renewed Framework objectives	**Focus on Contrast** **Y3 Strand 1: 3** Sustain conversation, explain or give reasons for their views or choices **Y3 Strand 8: 3** Identify features that writers use to provoke readers' reactions	**Focus on Characters** **Y3 Strand 3: 3** Use the language of possibility to investigate and reflect on feelings, behaviour or relationships **Y3 Strand 7: 2** Infer characters' feelings in fiction and consequences in logical explanations **Writing** **Y3 Strand 10: 2** Group related material into paragraphs

How to use the Navigator Fiction Teaching Guides

The *Navigator* Teaching Guides offer flexible routes through the stories for guided reading. The Guides put you in control of guided reading, as you choose the routes through the material depending on the needs of your children. Each session can be held over one or two days, as fits your timetable and the progress of your guided reading groups.

Session 1 / 2

At a Glance
This section will save you valuable time, by giving an overview of the story as well as highlighting the literacy opportunities in the text.

Independent reading
Depending on a group's ability, some children may be able to read the story ahead of the guided reading session. This section contains ideas of areas children could look out for or focus on as they read the text.

Text introduction
This short, focused section introduces the story to the children, and activates the prior knowledge and experience that they bring to the reading.

Teaching strategies
During this part of the session, children are supported in their reading and response to the text.
- **Question prompts:** These questions enable the teacher to assess whether children have understood the story. Also modelled are prompts to encourage children to question for themselves, such as 'Perhaps … ' and 'I wonder … '.
- **Going deeper:** These focused questions lead the children deeper into the text. They must support their views with evidence from the text. These sections encourage children to develop a range of comprehension skills:
  - Prediction: encouraging children to use their knowledge of the story so far to predict what might happen next.
  - Constructing images: asking children to visualise what is happening in the story, leading them to a close analysis of the text.

- Questioning: modelling questions that children might ask of each other, the author, or themselves.
- Text-structure analysis: expanding children's awareness of how texts are structured.
- Sequencing texts: applying knowledge about how texts are put together.
- Semantic strategies: supporting children in decoding unfamiliar words.
- Interpretive strategies: enhancing critical analysis skills, including inference and deduction, and reading between the lines.
- Monitoring understanding: encouraging children to reflect on their own understanding of the text.
- **Focus on:** This section focuses on a number of pages in the story and fulfils a key objective. Often this focused questioning requires children to read between and beyond the lines of the text.

Respond and return
Now the children reflect in detail on the text they have read. This is also an opportunity to consolidate the strategies used.

Follow-up
The PCM relates to both the Going deeper and Focus on sections, and has a reading focus.

Challenge: Differentiation
The main stem of the session is the same for all children. You can choose from the range of literacy activities available according to the group you are taking. As a guided reading session progresses faster with more able children, the Challenge sections extend the main stem of the session and build on the teaching that has gone before.

Session 3 / 4

Session 3 / 4 works in the same way as Session 1 / 2, but has a different learning objective and also focuses on a key writing objective. Depending on how fast children progress, you could ask them to complete the follow-up PCM (which always has a writing focus) in the next session. Additional writing suggestions are also given.

Activates children's prior knowledge

A focused look at the text

Allows teachers to check comprehension and facilitate group discussion

Story synopsis

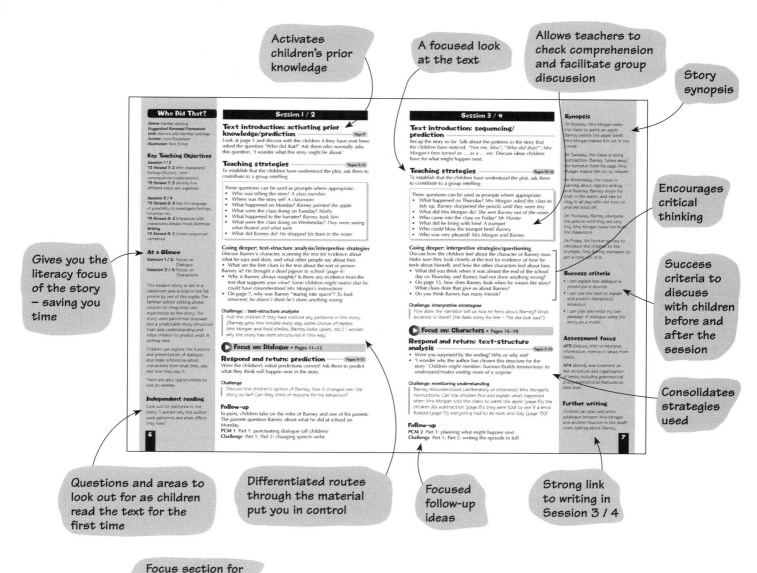

Gives you the literacy focus of the story – saving you time

Encourages critical thinking

Success criteria to discuss with children before and after the session

Consolidates strategies used

Questions and areas to look out for as children read the text for the first time

Differentiated routes through the material put you in control

Focused follow-up ideas

Strong link to writing in Session 3 / 4

Focus section for both sessions

Focused question prompts

Annotated pages put you in control

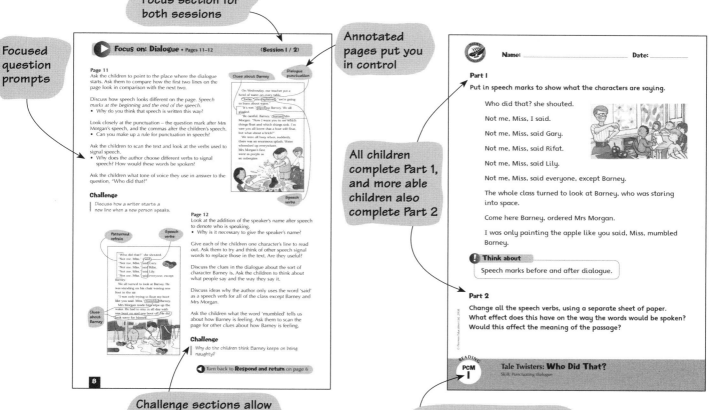

All children complete Part 1, and more able children also complete Part 2

Challenge sections allow more able children to go even deeper into the text

One reading and one writing copymaster for each story

Genre: Mystery stories
**Suggested Renewed Framework
Unit:** Adventure and mystery
Author: Paul Stewart
Illustrator: Tim Beer

Key Teaching Objectives

Session 1 / 2
Y3 Strand 7: 2 Infer characters' feelings (fiction) / infer consequences (explanations)
Y3 Strand 8: 3 Look at writers' craft

Session 3 / 4
Y3 Strand 1: 3 Sustain conversation; justify views
Y3 Strand 7: 1 Identify key points
Writing
Y3 Strand 10: 1 Write in coherent structure, using sequence, place and time

At a Glance

Session 1 / 2: Focus on 3rd Person Accounts
Session 3 / 4: Focus on Plot

A modern story, with strong descriptive writing, told in the 3rd person. Exploring how it might be seen through Jamie's eyes leads to work on comparing 1st and 3rd person accounts.

Mystery is built up from the start – finding the 'coin', seeing the girl 'dancing', being unable to move properly, and then the girl disappearing – providing a good model of the genre and offering opportunities for prediction. The author does not reveal that the coin lets Jamie see into the future until the climax of the story, so the children can search for clues.

The contrast between normality and when Jamie is looking into the future is an interesting aspect to explore.

Independent reading

How does the author create an atmosphere of mystery? 'I wonder what clues he will give us.'

Text introduction: prediction/ activating prior knowledge — Page 3

Look at page 3. Discuss what clues the title and the artwork give about the story. Ask if the children have ever been metal detecting.

Teaching strategies — Pages 3–13

To establish that the children have understood the plot, ask them to contribute to a group retelling.

These questions can be used as prompts where appropriate:
- What did Jamie like to spend his time doing? *Scratting – using a metal detector*
- What did Jamie find on Sunday? *A silver coin*
- What did he see at 9:45? *A dog barking and a girl dancing*
- As he went over to the girl, what happened? *She stopped moving and lay on the ground*
- What happened when Jamie knelt beside her? *She disappeared*
- What did Grandpa Davy think the coin was? *A talisman*

Going deeper: interpretive strategies/questioning

Discuss the use of the 3rd person to tell the story. Make sure the children scan the text for evidence.
- Does the narrator tell us any more or less than Jamie would have done at the start of the story?
- How does the narrator build the atmosphere? *'There was something there'; 'His heart missed a beat'; finding the coin*

Look for personal and possessive pronouns on pages 6–7. *He and his*
- If Jamie were a girl, what pronouns would the author use? *She and her*
- If Jamie were telling the story, what pronouns would he use? *I and my*

Challenge: interpretive strategies
How would the story be different if it were told by Jamie? Discuss any ideas the children have, e.g. point of view, feelings, language.

▶ **Focus on: 3rd Person Accounts • Pages 8, 10–11**

Respond and return: prediction — Pages 3–13

Discuss how successful the author has been at building up the feeling of mystery in the story. 'I wonder what will happen next.'

Challenge: questioning
Do the children think the story would have been better if it had been told in the 1st person? Why?

Follow-up

Ask children to make a list of ideas about what the numbers 1553 could be, and come back to it when they have read the rest of the story. Was the correct answer among their ideas?
PCM 1 Part 1: personal and possessive pronouns (all children)
Challenge Part 1; Part 2: writing a 1st person account

Text introduction: monitoring understanding/sequencing
Page 14

Ask one member of the group to recap the story so far. Write down the main points of the sequence: Jamie finds a coin/he sees a girl dancing/his grandpa suggests it is a talisman.

Teaching strategies
Pages 14–18

To establish that the children have understood the plot, ask them to contribute to a group retelling.

> These questions can be used as prompts where appropriate:
> • What happened on Monday after school? *Jamie went back to the mudflats. He realised that the high tide that day and the numbers on the coin were the same –1553*
> • What did he see? *He saw the dog jump into the river and the girl jump in after it*
> • What did Jamie realise? *He had seen the future*
> • What did he do? *He jumped in and saved her*
> • What happened to the talisman? *The numbers had changed to 1249*

Going deeper: text-structure analysis/inference
Discuss with the children how the author has carefully sequenced the story to build the mystery:
• Ask the children to point to the place in the text where the mystery starts to be resolved. *'He gasped. 1553!' (page 15)*
• Discuss why this is a significant part of the story.
• How does Jamie feel? Discuss the use of the verb 'gasped'.
• Do they find the story believable?

Challenge: questioning
Ask the group if they agreed with Jamie on page 14, 'no one can see into the future'. Discuss how the reader now expects the coin to be more than just a coin, because this is a mystery story.

 Focus on: Plot • Pages 16–18

Respond and return: text-structure analysis/inference
Pages 3–18

Look at the end of the mystery sequence: Jamie understands what the numbers on the coin mean/he sees the dog and the girl/he saves the girl/the numbers on the coin change. Discuss how life could become difficult for Jamie. What do they think Jamie might do with the coin? What do they think will happen at 12:49?

Challenge: deduction
Jamie says that the girl would not believe him if he told her about the coin. Discuss if the children think Grandpa Davy would believe Jamie. Make sure they use evidence from the text.

Follow-up
PCM 2 Part 1: sequencing the story (all children)
Challenge Part 1; Part 2: writing a 1st person account

Synopsis
Jamie spends much of his time with a metal detector, scouring the mudflats for treasure. One Sunday, he discovers an old coin inscribed with what he believes is the date 1553. Then he sees a dog, and a young girl who seems to dance before lying on the ground. Jamie closes his eyes and breathes deeply. When he opens his eyes, the girl has gone.

Grandpa Davy examines the coin. It is a talisman with the words 'The future is mine'.

On Monday after school, Jamie visits the mudflats. He arrives at almost 15:50 and remembers that high tide that day is 15:53 – the numbers on the talisman! He hears the dog and sees it jump into the river. The girl follows and Jamie realises that what he saw yesterday was, in fact, the future. He saves the girl from drowning. When he next looks at the coin, the numbers read 1249.

Success criteria
• I can discuss characters' feelings using evidence from the text.
• I can retell main points of a story in sequence.
• I can write a coherent 1st person account.

Assessment focus
AF3 Deduce, infer or interpret information, events or ideas from texts.

AF4 Identify and comment on the structure and organisation of texts, including grammatical and presentational features at text level.

Further writing
Plan and write a story in the 3rd person about what happens to Jamie at 12:49.

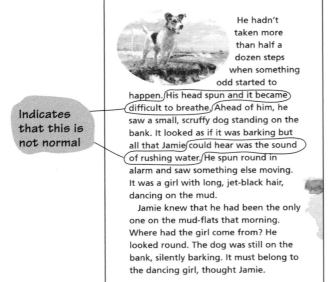

He hadn't taken more than half a dozen steps when something odd started to happen. His head spun and it became difficult to breathe. Ahead of him, he saw a small, scruffy dog standing on the bank. It looked as if it was barking but all that Jamie could hear was the sound of rushing water. He spun round in alarm and saw something else moving. It was a girl with long, jet-black hair, dancing on the mud.

Jamie knew that he had been the only one on the mud-flats that morning. Where had the girl come from? He looked round. The dog was still on the bank, silently barking. It must belong to the dancing girl, thought Jamie.

Indicates that this is not normal

8

Page 8

Discuss what difference, if any, it makes that 'Time and Tide' is written in the 3rd person. What more or less would we know if this was a 1st person account?

Discuss the strange things that happened to Jamie, i.e. head spinning/difficulty breathing/ hearing sound of rushing water. Discuss how this makes the reader aware that something strange is happening.

Pages 10–11

Ask the children to scan the text and point to all the personal and possessive pronouns. Ask the children what would happen if the author had not used any pronouns, and repeated 'Jamie' or 'the girl'.

Discuss how the author uses good descriptive language when he describes how Jamie walks – 'It was like wading through syrup.' Discuss what this would feel and look like. If this was a 1st person account, would Jamie have described it the same way?

Discuss the strange things that Jamie saw. Make sure the children use evidence from the text to back up their arguments.

• What do you think was happening?
• Was the girl really dancing?
• Do you think the dog and the girl were real up to the point when the girl disappeared?
• What do you think was making Jamie feel so strange?

Challenge

Explain that, often, writers put things in stories which are not explained until much later. Why do the children think writers do this?

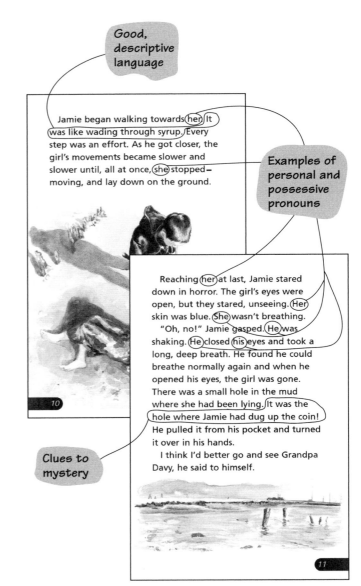

Good, descriptive language

Jamie began walking towards her. It was like wading through syrup. Every step was an effort. As he got closer, the girl's movements became slower and slower until, all at once, she stopped moving, and lay down on the ground.

Examples of personal and possessive pronouns

10

Reaching her at last, Jamie stared down in horror. The girl's eyes were open, but they stared, unseeing. Her skin was blue. She wasn't breathing.
"Oh, no!" Jamie gasped. He was shaking. He closed his eyes and took a long, deep breath. He found he could breathe normally again and when he opened his eyes, the girl was gone. There was a small hole in the mud where she had been lying. It was the hole where Jamie had dug up the coin! He pulled it from his pocket and turned it over in his hands.
I think I'd better go and see Grandpa Davy, he said to himself.

Clues to mystery

11

◀ Turn back to **Respond and return** on page 6

Page 16
Ask the children to explain how the author builds up the tension towards the climax of the story.

Can the children explain why the author has used capital letters when Jamie is shouting? Discuss the use of capitals to emphasise the danger.

Challenge

Ask the children to tell you if they have noticed any repeated phrases in the story: 'heart missed a beat'. Why do they think the author has repeated the same line? (Some children may say that it is to underline the fact that Jamie has already been through this once before.)

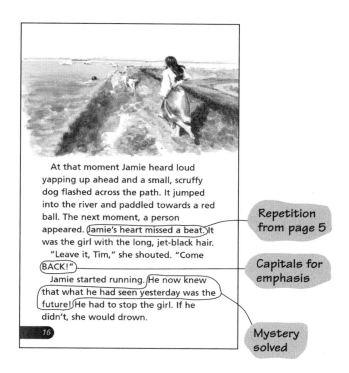

> At that moment Jamie heard loud yapping up ahead and a small, scruffy dog flashed across the path. It jumped into the river and paddled towards a red ball. The next moment, a person appeared. Jamie's heart missed a beat. It was the girl with the long, jet-black hair.
> "Leave it, Tim," she shouted. "Come BACK!"
> Jamie started running. He now knew that what he had seen yesterday was the future! He had to stop the girl. If he didn't, she would drown.

16

Repetition from page 5

Capitals for emphasis

Mystery solved

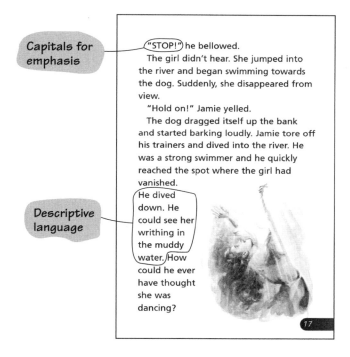

Capitals for emphasis

> "STOP!" he bellowed.
> The girl didn't hear. She jumped into the river and began swimming towards the dog. Suddenly, she disappeared from view.
> "Hold on!" Jamie yelled.
> The dog dragged itself up the bank and started barking loudly. Jamie tore off his trainers and dived into the river. He was a strong swimmer and he quickly reached the spot where the girl had vanished.
> He dived down. He could see her writhing in the muddy water. How could he ever have thought she was dancing?

17

Descriptive language

Page 17
Discuss how the children felt when the girl jumped into the water and disappeared.

Were the children surprised that Jamie rescued the girl? Discuss how we are led to expect that Jamie would save the girl.

Ask the children if they think that Jamie should have jumped in.

Page 18
Ask the children to retell the sequence at the end of the story: Jamie understands what the numbers on the coin mean/he sees the dog and the girl/he saves the girl/the numbers on the coin change.

Discuss the use of a cliffhanger ending with the children – what effect does it have on the reader? Why is it useful for the writer? What did they think when the number on the coin changed?

> Jamie grabbed her under her arms, kicked up and pulled her to the surface. The girl spluttered. Jamie twisted her round and held onto her tightly. He began swimming back to the bank.
> "You saved my life," the girl gasped.
> "I...I was just in the right place at the right time," he said. He didn't tell her why. She would not have believed him.
> ★ ★ ★
> When he got home, he pulled the talisman from his pocket. He looked at it and gasped.
> "1249," he said and shuddered. What was going to happen at 12:49?

18

Mystery not solved

Turn back to **Respond and return** on page 7 ◀

Part I

Put the correct personal or possessive pronoun in the gaps. Try not to look at the story.

❶ Jamie was really keen on metal detecting. _____ Grandpa Davy had shown _____ how a few years ago.

❷ Jamie peered into the hole. There was a glint of metal. _____ heart missed a beat.

❸ _____ reached down and scraped at the object with _____ fingernails.

❹ "A coin," said Jamie excitedly. _____ wiped _____ on _____ jeans.

❺ Jamie watched the girl spring upwards. _____ legs kicked wildly. _____ body twisted and _____ arms reached for the sky.

❻ Reaching _____ at last, Jamie stared down in horror. The girl's eyes were open, but they stared, unseeing. _____ skin was blue. _____ wasn't breathing.

Part 2

Imagine that you are Jamie. Put yourself into the story opening and, on a separate sheet of paper, retell the first paragraph in the 1st person:

Jamie was really keen on metal detecting. His Grandpa Davy had shown him how a few years ago. Scratting, he called it. For as far back as Jamie could remember, his grandfather had spent all his free time tramping up and down the mud-flats at low tide. The old man had a fine haul of medals, coins, jewellery, and a pewter mug which he had found. Like his grandpa, Jamie now spent all his spare time on the mud-flats of the river looking for treasure.

Name: _____ **Date:** _____

Part 1

Here are the events which happened at the end of the story but they are in the wrong order. Number the events in the correct order.

Event	Order
The girl jumped into the river.	☐
Jamie saw the girl with long, jet-black hair running after the dog.	☐
Jamie realised it was almost 15:53.	☐
Jamie managed to get her to the bank.	☐
Jamie shouted for the girl to stop.	☐
He heard the dog barking and saw it jump into the river.	☐
Jamie arrived at the mud-flats.	☐
Jamie realised what he had seen yesterday was the future!	☐
Jamie looked at the coin and saw that the numbers had changed!	☐
Jamie dived in after the girl.	☐

Part 2

Now write this part of the story as if it happened to you.

 Think about

Adding your feelings as things happen.

© Pearson Education Ltd, 2008

Spooky or What? Time and Tide
Skill: Sequencing

WRITING

PCM
2

The Girl in the Red Coat

Genre: Mystery stories
Suggested Renewed Framework
Unit: Adventure and mystery
Author: Sean Taylor
Illustrator: Hemesh Alles

Key Teaching Objectives

Session 1 / 2
Y3 Strand 3: 2 Work effectively with all group members
Y3 Strand 8: 3 Look at writers' craft

Session 3 / 4
Y3 Strand 7: 1 Identify key points
Y3 Strand 7: 2 Infer characters' feelings (fiction) / infer consequences (explanations)
Writing
Y3 Strand 9: 1 Create / evaluate their own writing

At a Glance

Session 1 / 2: Focus on Significant Aspects of the Story

Session 3 / 4: Focus on 1st Person Accounts

Set in 19th century London, this is a 1st person account told by a doctor. The setting reflects the living conditions of the time, including the prevalence of typhoid.

The atmosphere is built up through the descriptions of the setting, and the little girl's strange movements. The author drops clues throughout the story that hint towards the girl being a ghost. However, few readers will pick this up immediately, so this is a story that requires revisiting.

Independent reading

'I wonder how the author will help us to build a mental image of setting and atmosphere.'

Session 1 / 2

Text introduction: activating prior knowledge
Page 19

Tell the children that the story is set in Victorian England. Ask if they know anything about the life of poor children at this time and if they have heard of the deadly disease, typhoid.

Teaching strategies
Pages 19–27

To establish that the children have understood the plot, ask them to contribute to a group retelling.

> These questions can be used as prompts where appropriate:
> - Who was knocking at the door? *A girl wearing a red coat*
> - What did the little girl want? *The doctor to visit her mother*
> - What did the girl do when the doctor tried to pat her on the head? *She ducked away*
> - What did the doctor suspect the mother had? *Typhoid*
> - What was surprising about the way the girl moved? *She seemed to glide over the uneven ground*
> - What happened at the end of the alley? *He lost sight of her*

Going deeper: constructing images/questioning
Look closely at the story opening and see what techniques the author uses to start to build up the mystery:
- How does the author get you hooked from the start? *Strong descriptions, interesting setting*
- Discuss the effect that using the 1st person has on the story. *We know how he is feeling – we are kept distant from the girl*
- What are the first clues that the girl is mysterious? *Pale lips; ducked away; he keeps losing sight of her*

Challenge: questioning
What techniques does the author use to evoke the feeling of mystery? *Bad weather; setting (both time and place); being woken in the middle of the night, confused and disorientated.*

 Focus on: Significant Aspects of the Story • Pages 25–27

Respond and return: interpretive strategies/prediction
Pages 19–27

Discuss what the children think about the opening and the build-up of mystery in the story. Ask them to predict what might happen next.

Challenge: activating prior knowledge
Does the story remind the children of any other books? Does this help them to predict what might happen next?

Follow-up
With one child chosen as scribe, children generate a list of questions about the rest of the story. After they've read the rest of the story, they should return to their list to see if their questions were answered.
PCM 3 Part 1: comprehension exercise (all children)
Challenge Part 1; Part 2: going deeper into comprehension

Text introduction: monitoring understanding/interpretive strategies — Page 27

Ask one member of the group to recap the story so far (including the setting).

Ask the children what opinion they have formed of the doctor so far. What evidence is this based on?

Teaching strategies — Pages 28–32

To establish that the children have understood the plot, ask them to contribute to a group retelling.

> These questions can be used as prompts where appropriate:
> - When the doctor examined the woman, what did he diagnose? *Typhoid*
> - What did the doctor recommend she do? *Leave London for a while*
> - When she thanked the doctor, who did he say she should be thanking? *Her daughter*
> - What did the woman say about her daughter? *She died of typhoid last week*
> - Why was the doctor confused? *The girl led him here*
> - When the woman fetched the red coat, what was strange about it? *It was dry*

Going deeper: activating prior knowledge/interpretive strategies

Discuss the dialogue in the story with the children. Ask them to tell you the rules for dialogue punctuation – speech marks, commas and capital letters. Remind them if necessary that a new speaker starts on a new line.

Ask them what they think the doctor might have said when he felt the coat. How would he have said it? Discuss with the children how we can guess what the doctor would say because we have learnt a lot about his character throughout the story.

Challenge: interpretive strategies
Ask the children how they think the girl's mother felt when the doctor told her the story.

 Focus on: 1st Person Accounts •
Pages 20, 22–24

Respond and return: questioning — Pages 19–32

Ask the children if they were surprised by the ending. Did they pick up on any clues that suggested the girl was a ghost? Ask the children to go on a clue hunt and scan the text to pick up clues.

Challenge: questioning
Discuss how credible the events of the story seem.

Follow-up
PCM 4 Part 1: writing a 1st person account (all children)
Challenge Part 1; Part 2: continuing the story

Synopsis

In London, in 1862, a young doctor is woken early by knocking on his front door. It is a cold, wet girl in a red coat. She pleads with him to come and treat her mother. On the way, the doctor asks the girl about her mother's illness and deduces she has typhoid. The doctor has to walk quickly to keep up with the girl. He stumbles over debris, but the girl seems to glide effortlessly over the uneven ground. At the entrance to a narrow alley, she disappears. He stumbles down the alley and finds himself outside a door.

A pale, young woman opens the door. He confirms that she has typhoid. He tells her to leave London and go to the country. When she thanks him, he says she should thank her daughter. The woman tells him her daughter recently died of typhoid. She shows him the girl's red coat, which is dry as a bone.

Success criteria
- I can identify aspects of the story that evoke the feeling of mystery.
- I can explain how a 1st person account helps to give us information about a character.
- I can write a 1st person account.

Assessment focus
AF3 Deduce, infer or interpret information, events or ideas from texts.

AF5 Explain and comment on writers' use of language, including grammatical and literary features at word and sentence level.

Further writing
Write a review of the story, expressing your personal feelings about it.

13

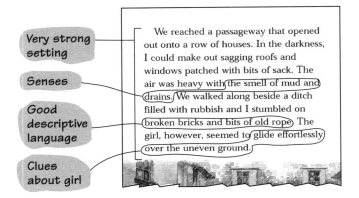

Very strong setting

Senses

Good descriptive language

Clues about girl

We reached a passageway that opened out onto a row of houses. In the darkness, I could make out sagging roofs and windows patched with bits of sack. The air was heavy with the smell of mud and drains. We walked along beside a ditch filled with rubbish and I stumbled on broken bricks and bits of old rope. The girl, however, seemed to glide effortlessly over the uneven ground.

Page 25
What clues are there in the text that this story is not set in the present day? How successful do the children think the author has been in setting this story in the past?

Ask the children to find examples of the author's use of descriptive language (language which creates a vivid picture in your mind):
• How successful has the author been at building up a mental picture?

Clues about the girl

Sets story in the past

The ditch had overflowed further up, and some rough planks had been put down here and there so that people could get across the mud. The girl knew her way better than I did. She hopped from one plank to the next, while I had to walk very carefully so as not to slip.
"It's a good thing we didn't come in that coach with four white horses!" I joked but the girl did not even look round.
"We're nearly there now!" I heard her call. "Our house is just up here!"

26

I reached the end of the planks and came to an alley between brick walls. I was pretty sure that was where the girl had gone but, when I peered down it, I could not see the red coat. All was darkness and rain.
I set off down the alley in any case, feeling my way along with a hand on the damp bricks. After only a few steps, I put my foot into a pot-hole that sent water sloshing over the top of my boot.
"Where are you?" I called after the girl. There was no reply but I kept going. I knew I must be close to where she lived. Not much further on, I found myself at the end of the alley. There was a door in the wall to my right but no sign of the girl. I remember tutting and wiping rain off my face before walking up to the door and knocking twice.

27

Clues about the girl

Senses

Page 26 and 27
Discuss how the setting comes alive, and how crucial it is to the atmosphere in the story. Can the children explain how the author has achieved this? Remind them to look for examples of sights, sounds, smells and touch.

Ask the children to look for clues about the girl in what she says and what she does. Discuss how the author is building up an air of mystery around the girl.

 Turn back to **Respond and return** on page 12

Discuss with the children how the 1st person account helps us learn a lot of information about the doctor from what he says and what he does. The author also gives us information through what the other characters say about him.

Ask the children what sort of man the doctor is. Ask one of them to find one piece of evidence in the text to support their view.

Explain to the children that you are going to look at how a character in a story is presented. Ask the children to scan the following pages to find information about the doctor:

• What do we learn about the doctor from what he tells us?
• What do we learn about the doctor from what other characters say?
• What do we learn about the doctor from what he says and does?

Young man

Kind man

Self aware

I will not forget that night. It was the autumn of 1862. I was a young doctor and had just started work in the East End of London. Behind my house, mile after mile of rickety slums and muddy alley-ways led down to the river. It was the poorest part of the city. Sometimes I would go to visit a family and find a mother, a father, a grandfather and four or five children all living in one room. It was hard for the families to find clean drinking water and so killer diseases were common. We doctors had our work cut out.

I pulled open the front door. Out in the street stood a girl with fair hair. She was wearing a red coat but was soaked to the skin, and I could tell from her pale lips that she was cold.

20

Before the clock had struck four, the girl and I were walking down the front steps of the house and out into the blustery darkness of the night.

"Now," I joked, "shall we take my coach with four white horses or shall we walk?"

The girl blinked up at me and said, "I bet you haven't got no coach and white horses!"

"You're right," I smiled. "Let's walk." I reached out a hand to pat her on the head but she ducked away. She jumped down the last steps and set off towards the river.

As I followed, I almost had to shout to make myself heard above the rain.

22

Sense of humour

Kind man

Practical

Caring man

"What's wrong with your mother?" I asked.

"She's gone terrible pale. She's got a headache. I don't know what's the matter."

She led me round the corner and down a narrow passageway.

"Is she coughing?" I asked, ducking under a washing-line strung between the walls.

"All the time. And she don't want to eat nothing."

I said nothing but my heart sank. The child's mother had all the symptoms of typhoid fever. It was the disease killing people right across London. Prince Albert, Queen Victoria's husband, had died of it only months before.

23

The little girl was some way ahead of me and I had to walk quickly to keep her in sight. All at once she stopped and turned back towards me.

"Is my mother going to die, Doctor?" she asked, looking at me with her clear eyes. "I heard that you was a good doctor. Can you save her?"

"Don't you worry," I said. "I'll do the best I can for her. That's a promise."

With that, she set off again and I hurriedly followed, so as not to lose her in the maze of alley-ways.

24

Reputation for being good

Kind man, tries to reassure girl

◀ Turn back to **Respond and return** on page 13

Name: _____ **Date:** _____

Part 1

Scan pages 19–25 and answer the questions below.

19 Write three adjectives which describe the knock on the door.

_____

20 'Behind my house, mile after mile of rickety slums and muddy alley-ways led down to the river.'
Why does the author choose those words to describe this part of London?

_____

23 The girl says that her mother is coughing all the time, "And she don't want to eat nothing."
How does the doctor feel when he hears this?

_____

Explain how you know.

_____

What other two symptoms does the girl's mother have?

_____

25 What clues does the author give us that there is something mysterious about the girl?

_____

Part 2

Answer these questions on a separate sheet of paper.

❶ What do you think about the girl? Is she mysterious? Give a reason for your answer.

❷ What did you think of the story opening? Did it make you want to go on reading?

READING

PCM 3

Spooky or What? The Girl in the Red Coat
Skill: Comprehension

Name: _____ **Date:** _____

Part 1

Rewrite the following two pages in the 1st person as if you are the girl's mother. Use a separate sheet of paper.

"Thank you, Doctor," she said in a hushed voice. "It could be worse news, then, couldn't it?"

"Quite so," I replied. "Don't thank me, though, thank that brave daughter of yours. If it hadn't been for her, I'm sure it would have been worse news."

"Daughter?" said the woman. "What do you mean?"

"The girl who came to fetch me."

"That wasn't my daughter," said the woman. "My daughter died. She died of typhoid. We buried her last week."

31

I was confused. "She knocked on my door less than an hour ago," I said. "She led me here . . . over the planks. She was wearing a red coat."

The woman put her hand up to her face. "That's not possible," she said. Then she got to her feet and walked over to a cupboard in the corner of the room. She pulled open the door and took out a red coat.

"This was my daughter's," she said with tears in her eyes.

I reached out my hand. The coat was as dry as a bone.

32

Part 2

Continue the story on a separate sheet of paper, where the doctor tells the girl's mother what has happened.

 Think about

Including:
The characters' feelings.
Speech verbs.
Dialogue rules.

© Pearson Education Ltd, 2008

Spooky or What? The Girl in the Red Coat
Skill: Writing a 1st person account

WRITING
PCM
4

Horses of the Winter Night

Genre: Mystery stories
Suggested Renewed Framework
Unit: Adventure and mystery
Author: David Clayton
Illustrator: Emma Shaw-Smith

Key Teaching Objectives

Session 1 / 2
Y3 Strand 1: 3 Sustain conversation; justify views
Y3 Strand 8: 3 Look at writers' craft

Session 3 / 4
Y3 Strand 3: 3 Use the language of possibility to investigate feelings, behaviour etc.
Y3 Strand 7: 2 Infer characters' feelings (fiction) / infer consequences (explanations)
Writing
Y3 Strand 10: 2 Use paragraphs

At a Glance

Session 1 / 2: Focus on Contrast
Session 3 / 4: Focus on Characters

A chaptered modern mystery told in the 3rd person. The author signals the horses' appearances by a change in the weather. This technique gives those episodes a feeling of mystery. During these violent changes in weather, Nick finds it hard to move – his body seems to move in slow motion. This use of contrast within the story is interesting to study.

Relationships between the characters can be plotted. Nick and Tom's relationship changes during the story. Page 39 hints that their mother knows something about the house the boys don't. The story leaves us with unanswered questions, providing opportunities for discussion.

Independent reading

Look out for the author's use of contrasts in the story. 'I wonder what effect this will have.'

18

Text introduction: prediction
Page 33

Look at the title and illustration on page 33. Discuss what they tell you about the story – they do not give the reader many clues. Then ask the children to read the title of Chapter 1 and the first line of the story – do they give any more clues?

Teaching strategies
Pages 33–41

To establish that children have understood the plot, ask them to contribute to a group retelling.

> These questions can be used as prompts where appropriate:
> * What did Nick notice while he was mopping the stable floor? *All the water vanished down a crack between two flagstones*
> * What did he find? *A secret space that smelled of hay*
> * What happened suddenly? *There was a raging snowstorm, he heard the horses and a voice shouting for help*
> * What happened when Nick was asleep? *He heard the voice*
> * What did Nick decide to do the next day? *Explore the area*
> * What did he do at midday? *He fell asleep*
> * What was the weather like when he woke up? *Dark clouds were racing across the sun*

Going deeper: questioning/sequencing

Discuss the significant aspects of the text so far:
* Does the opening of the story make you think this is a mystery story? What clues are there? *An old house, a dense wood*
* Would we know more about Nick's feelings if it were written in the 1st person? Why?
* Discuss the main incidents in the story so far. Discuss how the tension has been built up over the three chapters, and the author's technique of using weather changes to signal mystery.

Challenge: interpretive strategies

'I wonder what the significance is of Mum coughing when she talks about the old man.'

▶ Focus on: Contrast • Pages 35–37

Respond and return: interpretive strategies/prediction
Pages 33–41

Discuss the author's technique of structuring his story around contrasts. Do the children think that this is a good technique? What do the children think will happen next? Why?

Challenge: deduction

Discuss with the children why the author has used capital letters when the voice cries out. (*Because he's shouting.*)

Follow-up

Children go on a 'descriptive language hunt', finding examples that refer to the senses. They can record these on a grid under the headings: sight, sound, smell and touch.
PCM 5 Part 1: analysing contrast in the story (all children)
Challenge Part 1; Part 2: analysing language choice

Text introduction: monitoring understanding/sequencing

Ask one member of the group to recap the story. Can they remember what technique the author used to show when things were and were not normal?

Tell the children that in this session you are going to look closely at the characters in the story, and what we find out about their feelings, behaviour and relationships.

Teaching strategies
Pages 42–48

To establish that the children have understood the plot, ask them to contribute to a group retelling.

> These questions can be used as prompts where appropriate:
> - What did Tom think the horses were trying to do? *Kill him*
> - What did Nick realise he had to do? *Feed the horses*
> - When the old man whistled, what did the horses do? *Stand as still as statues*
> - What happened to the old man and the horses at the end? *They melted away*

Going deeper: inference/deduction
Discuss the character of Nick at the beginning of the story:
- Ask the children to go back to the beginning and find three bits of evidence to support their view. *The children might say: he likes to have friends around him, he is lonely and bored, he is close to his mother, he is helpful (unlike his brother)*
- Ask the children how they found out these facts about Nick. Discuss how we can find out about characters in a story – what they say and do; what others say and do to them.

Challenge: inference
Reread page 42. 'I wonder how Tom is feeling.' Discuss the various ways the author shows us.

 Focus on: Characters • Pages 38–39, 42, 48

Respond and return: interpretive strategies
Pages 33–48

Discuss how there are still unsolved parts of the story at the end. 'I wonder why the author has ended the story in this way.'
- Are you convinced that the old man and the horses will never come back? Why?
- What do you think about Nick's behaviour? Would you have acted like Nick or like Tom?

Challenge: questioning
The mystery of the horses is never really explained in the story. 'I wonder what the story is behind the mystery.'

Follow-up
PCM 6 Part 1: planning the first two paragraphs of a story (all children)
Challenge Part 1; Part 2: writing the first two paragraphs

Synopsis
Nick, his brother Tom, and their mother have moved to an old house in the country. One day, as Nick is mopping the stable floor, he notices the water running down a crack. He lifts a flagstone to find a place in which he can smell hay. Immediately the air turns icy and a snowstorm rages. With difficulty, Nick heads back to the house and then hears horses and a voice asking for help. Suddenly, everything is back to normal.

The next day is hot and sunny. Nick falls asleep under a tree. When he wakes, the weather has changed. He senses something is wrong and rushes home. The horses are back and Tom admits he lifted the stone. Nick follows the lead stallion into the stable and yells for help. An old man appears and whistles at the horses, making them still. The boys raise the flagstone and feed the hay to the horses. The sun comes back out, the old man raises his hand in thanks, and he and the horses disappear forever.

Success criteria
- I can explain how language is used to create contrasts.
- I can use the text to infer characters' feelings.
- I can plan and write the opening paragraphs of a story.

Assessment focus
AF3 Deduce, infer or interpret information, events or ideas from texts.

AF5 Explain and comment on writers' use of language, including grammatical and literary features at word and sentence level.

Further writing
Plan and write an extended mystery story, in which the old man and horses return.

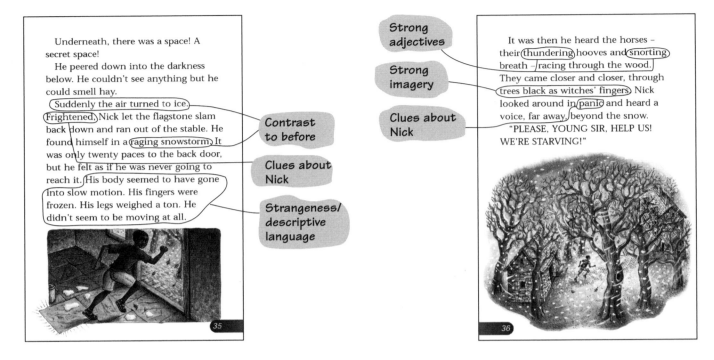

Underneath, there was a space! A secret space!

He peered down into the darkness below. He couldn't see anything but he could smell hay.

Suddenly the air turned to ice. Frightened, Nick let the flagstone slam back down and ran out of the stable. He found himself in a raging snowstorm. It was only twenty paces to the back door, but he felt as if he was never going to reach it. His body seemed to have gone into slow motion. His fingers were frozen. His legs weighed a ton. He didn't seem to be moving at all.

Contrast to before

Clues about Nick

Strangeness/ descriptive language

Strong adjectives

Strong imagery

Clues about Nick

It was then he heard the horses – their thundering hooves and snorting breath – racing through the wood. They came closer and closer, through trees black as witches' fingers. Nick looked around in panic and heard a voice, far away, beyond the snow.

"PLEASE, YOUNG SIR, HELP US! WE'RE STARVING!"

Pages 35–36

Explain to the children that you are going to be looking at contrast in the story, how this works and why it makes the story feel strange. You are also going to look at the author's use of language to create these effects.

Remind the children of the opening phrase of the story: *One hot summer*

Ask the children to point out where the contrast in the weather starts. Discuss how it is completely opposite from the weather Nick experienced previously.

- What else shows that this weather change is not normal? *Nick's movements/feels cold*
- Look at the adjectives the author uses to describe the scene – how useful are they?

Page 37

Look closely at the author's choice of language to describe the contrasting scene. Discuss the use of powerful verbs (*slipped down; cast*) and adjectives (*shimmering; towering; long*) to describe the scene. Ask the children to search the page for the best verbs and adjectives.

Discuss with the children how the weather changes when everything is back to normal.

Challenge

Why do the children think the author has used this technique? *Some children might say it's very atmospheric, feels like a different world, weather matches feelings*

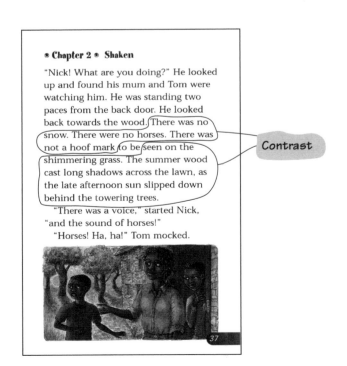

● Chapter 2 ● Shaken

"Nick! What are you doing?" He looked up and found his mum and Tom were watching him. He was standing two paces from the back door. He looked back towards the wood. There was no snow. There were no horses. There was not a hoof mark to be seen on the shimmering grass. The summer wood cast long shadows across the lawn, as the late afternoon sun slipped down behind the towering trees.

"There was a voice," started Nick, "and the sound of horses!"

"Horses! Ha, ha!" Tom mocked.

Contrast

◀ Turn back to **Respond and return** on page 18

Pages 38–39

Remind the children to look at what the characters say and do, and what they say and do to each other. Ask the children to scan pages 38 and 39 and find clues in the text to tell you about:

• Nick
• Tom
• their mother

Now ask the children to think about the characters' relationships with each other – what evidence is there in the text?

Challenge

Ask the children to think about why Nick's mother coughs when describing the previous owner. What is the author trying to suggest to us here?

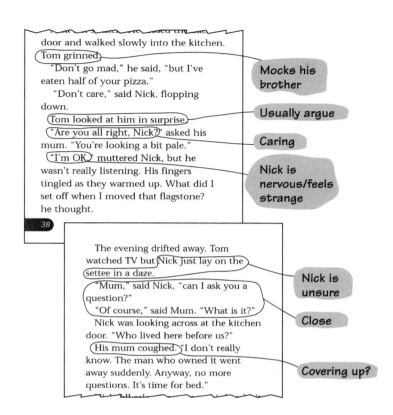

door and walked slowly into the kitchen.
Tom grinned. — *Mocks his brother*
"Don't go mad," he said, "but I've eaten half of your pizza."
"Don't care," said Nick, flopping down.
Tom looked at him in surprise. — *Usually argue*
"Are you all right, Nick?" asked his mum. "You're looking a bit pale." — *Caring*
"I'm OK," muttered Nick, but he wasn't really listening. His fingers tingled as they warmed up. What did I set off when I moved that flagstone? he thought. — *Nick is nervous/feels strange*

38

The evening drifted away. Tom watched TV but **Nick just lay on the settee in a daze.** — *Nick is unsure*
"Mum," said Nick, "can I ask you a question?"
"Of course," said Mum. "What is it?" — *Close*
Nick was looking across at the kitchen door. "Who lived here before us?"
His mum coughed. "I don't really know. The man who owned it went away suddenly. Anyway, no more questions. It's time for bed." — *Covering up?*

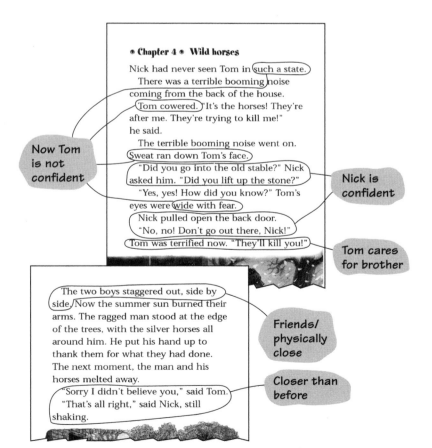

⊕ **Chapter 4** ⊕ **Wild horses**

Nick had never seen Tom in **such a state.**
There was a terrible booming noise coming from the back of the house. — *Now Tom is not confident*
Tom cowered. "It's the horses! They're after me. They're trying to kill me!" he said.
The terrible booming noise went on.
Sweat ran down Tom's face.
"Did you go into the old stable?" Nick asked him. "Did you lift up the stone?" — *Nick is confident*
"Yes, yes! How did you know?" Tom's eyes were **wide with fear.**
Nick pulled open the back door.
"No, no! Don't go out there, Nick!"
Tom was terrified now. "They'll kill you!" — *Tom cares for brother*

The two boys staggered out, side by side. Now the summer sun burned their arms. The ragged man stood at the edge of the trees, with the silver horses all around him. He put his hand up to thank them for what they had done. The next moment, the man and his horses melted away. — *Friends/ physically close*
"Sorry I didn't believe you," said Tom.
"That's all right," said Nick, still shaking. — *Closer than before*

Pages 42 and 48

Discuss how Nick and Tom's feelings have swapped over during the story:

• How is Nick feeling now? What evidence is there?
• How is Tom feeling now? What evidence is there?

By the end of the story, ask the children to find evidence to show that their relationship has changed. Do the children think that the boys' relationship will always be like this?

◀ Turn back to **Respond and return** on page 19

Part I

Go back and read pages 33–41 again. Now write down the words which show the contrast between the following:

Town	Country
_____ _____	_____ _____
_____ _____	_____ _____
_____ _____	_____ _____

Tom	Nick
_____ _____	_____ _____
_____ _____	_____ _____
_____ _____	_____ _____

Weather when everything is normal	Weather when everything is strange
_____ _____	_____ _____
_____ _____	_____ _____

Part 2

"It was then he heard the horses – their thundering hooves and snorting breath – racing through the wood. They came closer and closer, through trees black as witches' fingers."

Why do you think the author chose those words to describe the horses? Explain your reasons on a separate sheet of paper.

READING

PCM 5

Spooky or What? Horses of the Winter Night
Skill: Analysing contrast

Name: _____ **Date:** _____

Part 1

You are going to plan the first two paragraphs of a story. Use this sheet for your planning.

In the first paragraph, everything is normal.

> _____
>
> _____
>
> _____

In the second paragraph, strange things begin happening.

> _____
>
> _____
>
> _____

! Think about

Where your story takes place.
Who the character in your story is.
What your character is doing.
Words you can use to describe when things are normal – first paragraph.
Words you can use to describe when things are strange – second paragraph.

Part 2

Now write the two paragraphs on a separate sheet of paper.

Spooky or What? Horses of the Winter Night
Skill: Writing story openings

WRITING
PCM
6

Rigby
Halley Court, Jordan Hill, Oxford, OX2 8EJ

Rigby is an imprint of Pearson Education Limited, a company incorporated in England and Wales, having its registered office at Edinburgh Gate, Harlow, Essex, CM20 2JE. Registered company number: 872828

www.rigbyed.co.uk

Rigby is a registered trademark of Reed Elsevier, Inc, licensed to Pearson Education Limited

Text © Pearson Education Limited 2008
Cover © David Kearney/Artist Partners Ltd and John Walker 2002

First published 2002
This edition first published 2008

12 11
10 9 8 7 6 5 4

British Library Cataloguing in Publication Data is available from the British Library on request.

ISBN 978 0 433 07888 3

Typeset by Red Giraffe
Illustrated by David Kearney (cover); Emma Shaw-Smith (pages 1, 20–21); Nick Schon (page 5); Tim Beer (pages 8–9); Hemesh Alles (pages 14–15, 17)
Logo artwork by Max Ellis
Printed in Malaysia, KHL-CTP

Every effort has been made to contact copyright holders of material reproduced in this book. Any omissions will be rectified in subsequent printings if notice is given to the publishers.